Dan

1757

by

Parrish Wells

The accompanying story is based upon contemporary letters and journals, both English and French, written by soldiers or officers in the last French and Indian War.

Chief among the French sources were "Voyage au Canada," by J. C. B.; Vol. XI of the Lévis Papers, edited by L'abbé Casgrain, and the reports of Pierre-Georges Roy, "L'archiviste de la Province de Québec" for 1923-24 and 1926-27.

THE AUTHOR

ISBN 0-9629159-0-4

1st Printing 1940
Free Press Printing Company
Burlington, Vermont

Reprint 1975
Acme Press
Schenectady, New York

Revised Edition 1991
Pine Tree Press
Rome, New York

About the Author . . .

James Parrish Wells was born November 12, 1890 in Johnstown, New York. He attended the University of Rochester where he graduated as a Civil Engineer and took extra courses at the University of Wisconsin and Cornell University. He worked for many years as a hydraulic engineer in Rochester, New York and put in many municipal water supplies throughout the State. In 1946, Mr. Wells and his family moved to Plattsburgh, New York where he remained until just before his death in October, 1963.

Mr. Wells had had for many years a great interest in the period of history called the French and Indian Wars. As his work took him to all parts of the state and beyond, he conducted an extensive research on this period of history whenever he had the opportunity. He visited many libraries and corresponded with those he was not able to visit. Many of his notes were obtained by reading old and obscure records and diaries.

Mr. Wells used this source material to write and publish "Dangerous Journeys," a factual account of two men engaged in the conflict, and the trials and tribulations in their escape from Fort Niagara and their journey to Fort William Henry. He also wrote two novels of this period called "50,000 Heroes" and "The Rocks Beneath Us" which were completed but not published. An extensive effort is now being made by his daughter, Marjorie Harrison, who now resides in Hackettstown, New Jersey, to get this material into print.

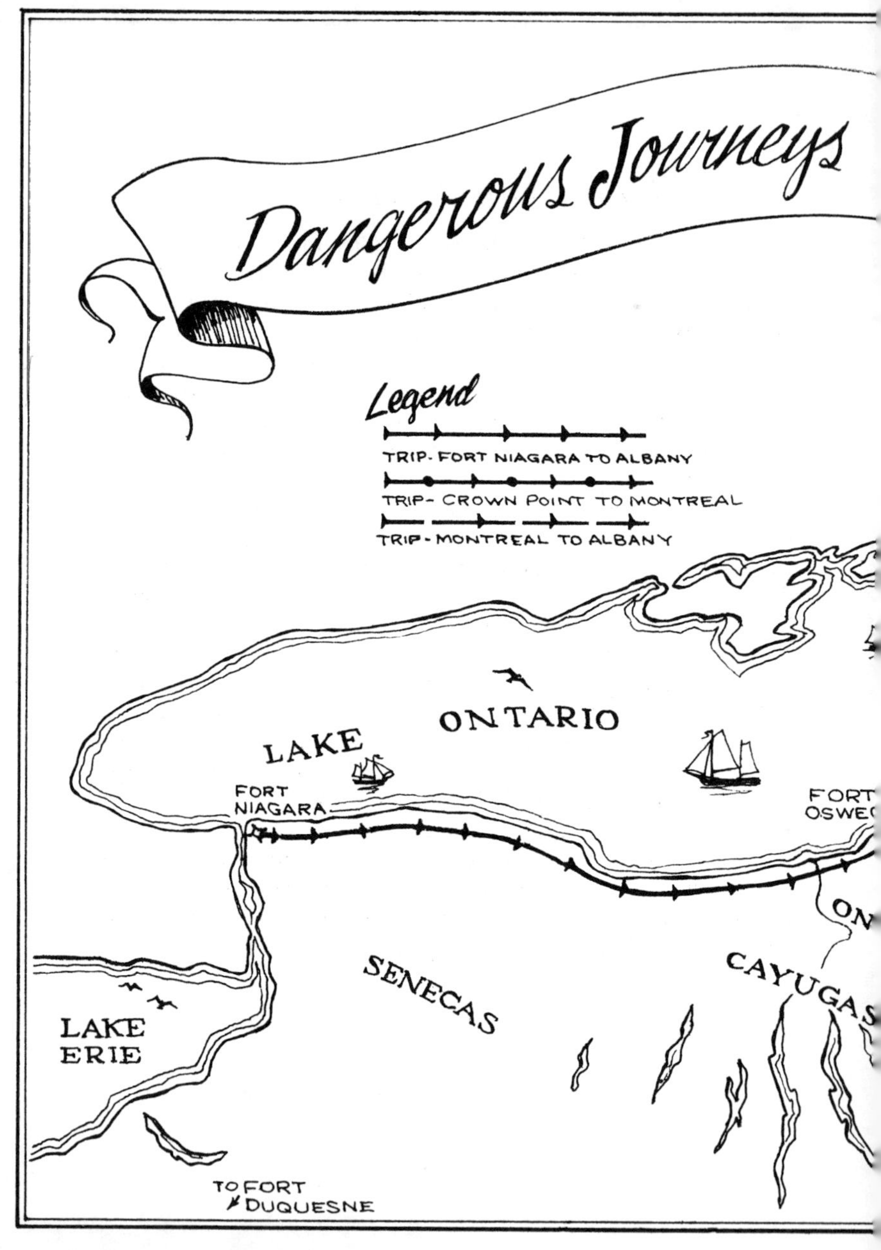

Dangerous Journeys

Legend
TRIP - FORT NIAGARA TO ALBANY
TRIP - CROWN POINT TO MONTREAL
TRIP - MONTREAL TO ALBANY

LAKE ONTARIO
FORT NIAGARA
FORT OSWEGO
LAKE ERIE
SENECAS
CAYUGAS
ON
TO FORT DUQUESNE

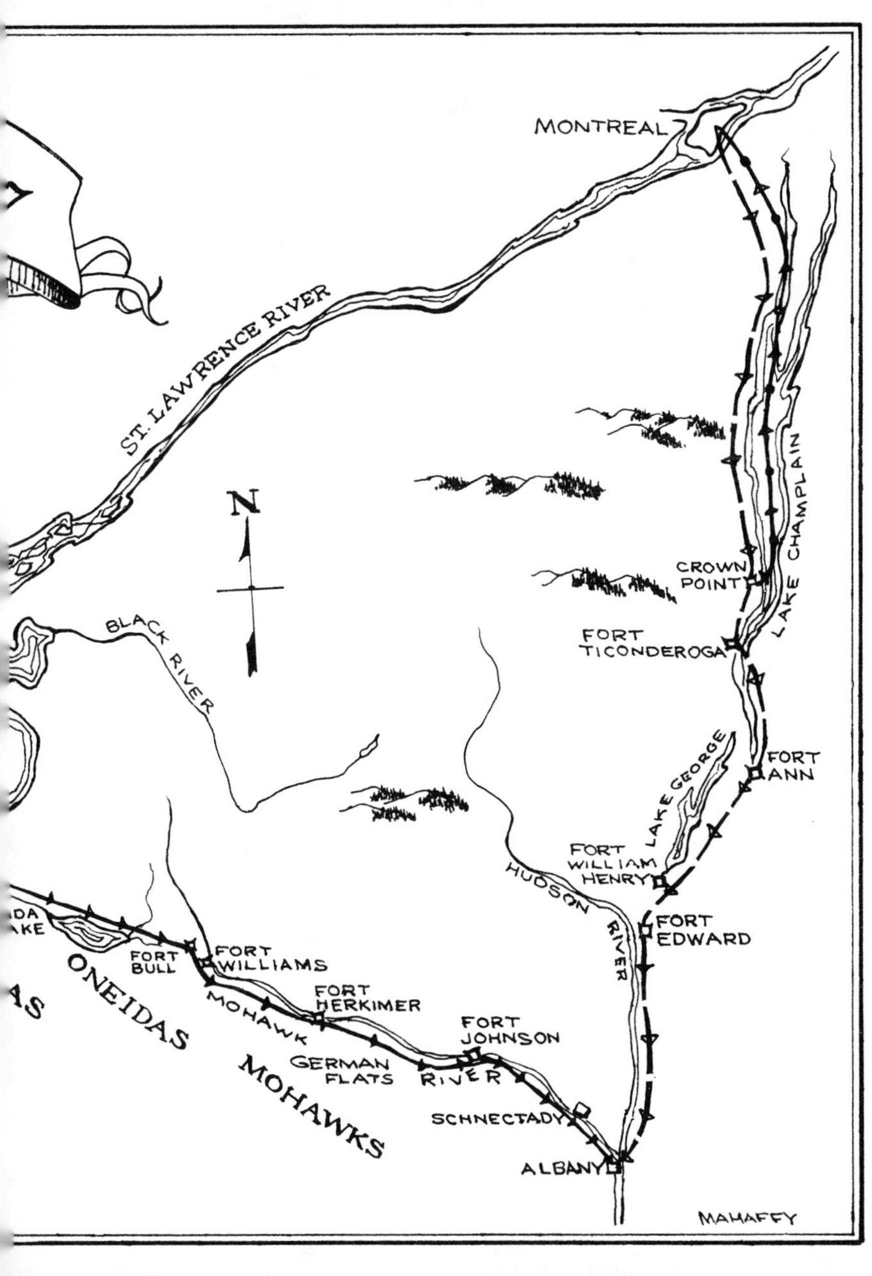

MONTREAL
ST. LAWRENCE RIVER
LAKE CHAMPLAIN
N
CROWN POINT
BLACK RIVER
FORT TICONDEROGA
LAKE GEORGE
FORT ANN
FORT WILLIAM HENRY
HUDSON RIVER
FORT EDWARD
FORT BULL
FORT WILLIAMS
ONEIDAS
MOHAWK
FORT HERKIMER
FORT JOHNSON
GERMAN FLATS
MOHAWKS
RIVER
SCHNECTADY
ALBANY
MAHAFFY

"Peter, I have seen all I want to of the French and these savages who are continually coming in with scalps of our people. What do you say, that this very night we start eastward, along the shores of Lake Ontario?"

The speaker, William Phelps, a ship carpenter from New York City, addressed his remarks to Peter Luney, the Virginian.

It was the middle of June in 1757. Both men were working on the east bank of the Niagara River, where it discharges the waters of the four other Great Lakes into Lake Ontario. Back of them was the French fort, commanded by Captain Pouchot. Though prisoners, they frequently worked outside of the walls of the fort.

Peter Luney had been captured in June of the previous year while defending "a block house in Virginia." He had been carried to Detroit, then inhabited by the French settlers, with many Indians living nearby. When the savages came to Niagara to trade they had brought Luney along with them.

In 1755, William Phelps had sailed up the Hudson from New York to Albany. From there he had gone overland to Schenectady, thence in a battoe up the Mohawk River to the carrying place, down Wood Creek to Oneida Lake, across that lake and down the river to Oswego, on Lake Ontario.

Phelps had been a member of the expedition, commanded by Governor Shirley of Massachusetts. Shirley was formerly an English lawyer. It had been his intention to continue up the shore of Lake Ontario to capture Niagara. Then with its garrison of only sixty men, its capture would have been an easy matter. Yet, late in October, Governor Shirley and his officers had decided not to go beyond Oswego. Phelps had remained to cut timber and work on the vessels.

With three others, Charles Carter of Philadelphia, James Flanagan and Lewis Dunning of New Jersey, he had been captured in May, 1756, while they were cutting timber in the woods outside of Oswego.

With their Indian captors they had started for Niagara. Dunning, unable to travel rapidly because of a wound, had been killed and scalped by the Indians. When the three remaining captives reached Niagara, Flanagan and Carter had been sent to Montreal. Phelps had been adopted by the savages and conducted to their country. Unable to prevail upon him to forget his own people and live contentedly with them, the Indians had returned him to Niagara. There Phelps had spent the winter.

For two or three minutes Peter Luney pondered the proposal of the New York man.

"You reckon you know the way?" he finally asked.

"All we have to do," said Phelps, "is to follow the shore of Lake Ontario, until we reach the mouth of the Oswego River. Then we follow up that river, and one of its branches, until we reach Oneida Lake. We can follow the shore of Oneida Lake to the mouth of Wood Creek, and go up that stream to what they call the Carrying Place. From there it's but a short distance to the Mohawk River. Then we follow the Mohawk until we reach German Flats, the Palatine village, or Fort Herkimer, which is across the river from it. Then we will be back among our own people."

"How far do you figure that is?" said Luney.

"Something like 250 miles, maybe more," said Phelps.

As they stood talking, a brig entered the mouth of the Niagara River from the lake.

"Of all things," said Phelps, "that's the very brig we built at Oswego. Montcalm must have captured it when he took the forts last year."

Not far behind the brig were two French schooners. All three vessels had come from Frontenac, that French post and fort directly north of Oswego, on the opposite shore of Lake Ontario. The three vessels had brought 280 of the Canadian militia to Niagara.

When the lake was free of ice, French vessels frequently plied between Niagara and Frontenac. When the lake was partly frozen over the hardy Frenchmen travelled on the ice along its shores. Winter had no terrors for the Canadians who came from Montreal and far-off Quebec.

"This wouldn't be a bad time to begin our journey," continued Phelps. "The garrison here will be occupied for the next two or three days in becoming acquainted with these newcomers and in hearing the news from Montreal and Quebec."

"Let's wait a day or two, and plan just how we'll do it," said Luney. "I had hoped," he continued, "that we would get a chance to go together to the great cataract up the river. We passed by it when the Indians brought me here. There was a French soldier in Fort Duquesne who told me that in April, 1753, he climbed down into the gorge, below the falls, and found a cavern back of the falling water. This Frenchman told me that he had asked others about it and as far as he knew he was the first white man to discover this cave."

"He must have had plenty of courage," said Phelps.

"Yes," said Luney. "Even though they are our enemies, the French have more than their share of courage. They are afraid of no hardships and the dangers of a new country like this mean nothing to them. No matter what the season of the year, they'll even brave the waters of these great lakes in their battoes in the middle of the winter. I took a look down into the gorge where he had told me he had gone down. The only things that I could see which he could have hung on to were a few small trees or shrubs which grew in the crevices of the rock. It took him an hour to get to the bottom. He said that this cave which he found, in back of the waterfall, he thought was about seventy feet wide, twenty feet high and about fifteen feet in depth.   He said that the noise in it was terrible and that even the rocks trembled from the impact of the falling water.   When he came to the top again he was deaf for two hours."

"Well, some time or other," said Phelps, "maybe after the war is over, we will have time enough to go and see the falls."

During the following two days Phelps and Luney learned all they could of the plans of the French for the coming summer.   If there was to be an invasion of the Mohawk Valley, their proposed journey would be of considerable danger and hardly worth the risk.

From such information as they were able to obtain, they concluded that the French military resources were to be employed in a campaign on Lake George.

The French Generals Montcalm, Levis and Bourlamaque were to lead an army of regulars, Canadians and savages against Fort William Henry.

Luney and Phelps, in their attempt to reach Fort Herkimer on the Mohawk River, would only have to avoid Indian scouting parties.   The danger from these would be great enough, but they would have to take the risk.

Two days after the three vessels had arrived from Frontenac, on Saturday the 18th of June, the two prisoners decided to begin their long journey eastward.

About midnight they made their way to the shore of Lake Ontario. To prevent the savages from following their tracks they had decided to walk through the water along the edge of the lake. They would travel at night and sleep in the woods during the day.

Unfortunately they had had no luck in obtaining provisions. From a drunken Indian they had taken a musket and about thirty charges of powder and ball.

Both men were in good physical condition. Luney had lived an outdoor life with the Indians. Phelps had been busy at his carpenter's trade. Luney was tall and lean and burned by the sun almost to the color of the savages. Phelps was fair haired and below the average height. What he lacked in height he made up for in width.

The travelling along the shore of the lake, keeping at all times in the water, would have been by no means easy, even in the daytime. At night it was very difficult. More than once they slipped, fell and were completely deluged by the waves which beat against the shore.

Before daylight they had covered only six miles of their journey. At the first sign of dawn they walked up the bed of a brook. About a hundred feet back from the shore they took off their wet clothing. Hanging their garments on some branches, they laid down on a bed of moss.

By noon, even though their laborious journey of the previous night had tired them to the point of needing many hours of sleep, the mosquitoes and flies had made it utterly impossible to continue their slumbers. They welcomed the protective covering of their dry clothing.

Their sole food for the day consisted of a few wintergreen leaves. As soon as it was dark they again began their journey. They had determined to spend one more night walking in the water. Having made an earlier start than on the previous night, before it was daylight they had covered ten more miles.

By this time both of them had begun to feel the pangs of hunger. Yet, to shoot off their gun would have been the height of folly. For all they knew, some of the enemy Indians might at that very moment be camped not far down the shore of the lake.

The two travellers spent the day on a point some twenty feet above the level of the lake. Here lying on their bellies, they could look out on the water without being seen.

"It was just as well we left the water," said Peter, not over five minutes after they had stretched themselves out on the leaves. "Look down the lake."

Phelps cautiously peered out. Coming along the shore, not over a half of a mile away, were two canoes each containing three occupants.

"They're going towards Niagara," said Phelps, "so they won't be looking for us."

Fully realizing the ability of the savages to see things entirely ignored by white men, the two fugitives retreated into the woods, praying that they had left no tracks along the shore. To their relief, the two canoes passed by at least a hundred yards out in the lake.

"Those savages," said Phelps, "are probably of the Six Nations on their way to Fort Niagara to obtain ammunition from Captain Pouchot at Fort Niagara. General Johnson has a very worthy antagonist in Captain Pouchot. The Indians all have a very high regard for the captain."

When Luney and Phelps again set out, under cover of the darkness, they found that they were on a beach, which alternated between sand and gravel.

"We can keep out of the water here," said Peter; "if we stay close to the edge of it the waves will soon wash away any tracks we leave."

That night they estimated that they had covered twenty miles. As this was their third night without food, their hunger had made them desperate. At the first signs of daylight they ceased their travelling.

"What's that smell, Peter?" said Phelps.

Luney went down the beach a hundred feet and returned with two fish.

"These are what you smelled, boy," he said. "I don't know about you, but I'm going to eat one of them."

"If you can, I can," said Phelps. "Maybe it's their guts that smell, and after we clean them they won't be so bad. Give me one of them."

They repaired to the woods with their treasures. With two sharp pointed sticks it took but a few minutes to clean the fish.

As Phelps had said, the worst of the smell came from their inwards. They soon had devoured both of them raw and in spite of the taste which unexpectedly they found, was worse than the smell.

"I hope they stay down," said Peter. "I never thought I'd get to the point that I'd eat raw fish, and spoiled besides."

After a quarter of an hour, having concluded that the fish were going to stay with them, they stretched themselves out on the ground and were almost immediately asleep.

When they awoke they judged from the position of the sun that it was about two hours before dark. Both of them felt refreshed from the food, such as it was; they had had their best sleep since beginning the journey.

"Peter," said Phelps, "from what I can remember of the country between Oswego and Niagara, we must be about half way to the river, which comes from the country of the Senecas. The French call the river the 'Cascouchiagon.' When we reach it, we'll have to swim it."

"Well, we can do it," said Luney. "We have already swam some small ones and I've swam the Potomac many a time, and it's a sizable river."

After two nights more of good travelling, but still with nothing more to eat, Phelps and Luney had reached the "Cascouchiagon." The faintest streak of daylight had appeared in the east.   In order that they might begin their march the next night with dry clothing, they decided to swim the river at once and to sleep on the opposite bank, while their clothes were drying.

They fastened their musket to a piece of drift wood.   As both were strong swimmers, they had no difficulty making the east bank of the river.

After they had slept five or six hours, they put on their dry clothing and looked about for food. The best the now almost famished travellers could find was some sassafras bark. When they returned to the edge of the woods they saw a young fawn, drinking on the shore of the lake.

"What do you say we shoot it?" said Luney.

"It isn't safe yet," said Phelps. "Three or four miles to the east of us is Irondequoit Bay. Many of the Seneca Indians enter Lake Ontario from it. Some of them use this river, though they have to go around the falls which are a few miles up the stream.

"Before Oswego fell," he continued, "we could count most of the Senecas as our allies. After the loss of Oswego it hasn't been certain much where they do stand. We had better not shoot anything until we are well to the eastward of Irondequoit Bay."

Luney had already lifted his gun to fire. He lowered it with some reluctance.

"I guess I can go through another day if you can," he said.

"I want to keep all the hair on my head," said Phelps. "You know as well as I do that some of these savages have unpleasant ways of putting their prisoners to death, particularly if some of their own warriors have been killed.

"I have no desire to be tied to a tree, dangling on hot coals, while Indian women push red hot bayonets into my nose and ears, and burn my finger tips in tobacco pipes, while their playful children shoot arrows into my legs and arms."

That night the two fugitives walked along an excellent sand beach, which extended from the Cascouchiagon River eastward for three or four miles. With considerable caution they proceeded along the bar separating Irondequoit Bay from the lake, for there was the possibility that some Indians might be camped upon the bar. Fortunately there were none.

With a few strong strokes they swam the outlet of the bay. Sometime after midnight they came to some bluffs along the shore and found the travelling none too good. At the first signs of daylight they climbed up onto a point that jutted out into the lake.

As soon as it was light they found that they could see several miles both to the east and to the west. They were soon asleep, but about noon their slumbers were interrupted by the beating of the waves on the shore. A heavy wind storm had come up and five- or six-foot waves were crashing against the foot of the bluff.

"With the noise of these waves," said Philip, "I think we could risk a shot with the musket, if we could find something to shoot."

"We're just as apt to see something if we stay where we are as if we move around," said Luney, as he made the musket ready to fire.

Both of them had become by now so weak that they were content to sit quietly and await their luck.

After two hours their patience was rewarded. Luney had sighted six wild turkeys not over a hundred feet away.

"If you never have prayed before, pray now, boy," said Luney as he raised his musket. He fired. One of the turkeys fluttered about and then lay still. Five minutes later Luney and Phelps were eagerly devouring its raw flesh.

"I never had anything taste better than this in my life," said Phelps.

"I'll admit it's somewhat better than raw fish," said the Virginian. "I've seen as many as a hundred and fifty of those birds roosting in one tree. The French hunted them around Presque Isle along the south shore of Lake Erie. They did their hunting on moonlight nights."

"Right now," said Phelps, "I'm satisfied to have only one of them."

The turkey was an unusually large one and after their repast more than half of it still remained.

"That will take us through tomorrow," said Luney. "How much further do you think it is to Oswego?"

"I'd say fifty miles or more," said Phelps. "With reasonably good walking along the beach we ought to make it in three nights."

As Phelps and Luney came nearer to Oswego they found the beach covered with large stones. The woods along the shore were full of oak and chestnut trees.

Phelps' estimate of the time that it would take them to reach Oswego had been correct. At the end of the third night he saw some familiar landmarks in the dim morning light, which caused him to say to his companion:

"It isn't over two miles to Oswego, Peter, let's get into the woods."

The two men left the lake shore, and after proceeding cautiously for not over an hour they reached the ruins of the picket fort on the hill above the site of Fort Oswego.

"Look here, man," said Phelps. "I was hoping we would find some of these and here they are."

"What have you found?" said Luney, who was fifty feet in the rear.

"Strawberries, and plenty of them," said Phelps.

The two hungry men wasted no further time in words, but devoured the delicious berries which grew in great abundance about the ruins of the stockaded fort.

"Eating these berries," said Phelps, "was one of the pleasant things about our stay here at Oswego. This seems to be one of the localities where they just grow naturally and there are several excellent varieties. We had plenty of fruit while we were here, and always good fishing."

"Can we take a chance on the Indians in this neighborhood?" said Luney.

"We can't be sure," replied Phelps. "If we meet any, they are apt to be Onondagas, Cayugas or Oneidas. There is no harm in our looking around here a bit," he continued, "as long as we keep back from the river."

Together they went down among the ruins of Fort Oswego.

"The French didn't leave much of it," said Luney.

"Indeed, they didn't," said Phelps. "Think of the work we did around this place and then to have to have the French destroy all our work in a few days and take all our supplies."

"That sort of thing has happened to quite an extent in this war," said the Virginian. "Think of the tremendous labor of Braddock's soldiers in bringing their supplies and artillery over the mountains of western Pennsylvania. After the French had given them a terrible beating, they simply took the English cannon and all their supplies and money. I've been told that the French used some of Braddock's cannon when they captured Oswego."

"As far as I could gather from what the French soldiers and Indians at Niagara told me," said Phelps, "the garrison, here at Oswego, didn't wake up to the fact that they were to be attacked until some men who had started down the lake came rowing back with the surprising news that a French army with artillery was camped on the shore of the lake, 'not over a mile and a half east of the forts.' "

"What consternation that must have caused," said Luney.

"Before they hardly had time to realize what had happened," said Phelps, "the French had attacked Fort Ontario, a picket fort, 205 feet on a side, located on the high ground across the river.

"As there weren't many of them, and the fort in ill condition to stand a siege, its garrison forded the river and came into Fort Oswego.

"Three days after they had first learned of the French camp down the lake, the English woke up in the morning to find an artillery battery on the other side of the river, already to send some shot into Fort Oswego.

"That's just what they did, too. One of the cannon balls killed Colonel Mercer, the commander. Shortly after that happened the rest of the officers held a council and decided to surrender.

It's too bad the garrison didn't put up more of a fight. Colonel Schuyler, in command of the Jersey Blues, shed tears, he was so mortified at the decision.

"When the white flag was raised over Fort Oswego, the Canadians and savages had crossed over to this side of the river. They soon would have been attacking Fort Oswego from the woods to the south. Colonel Schuyler was in Fort George, the picket fort, where we found the strawberries. He was about to make a sortie with the Jersey Blues."

"What happened to the garrison?" said Luney.

"A few of them," replied Phelps, "tried to get away in the woods, but the Indians caught most of those and scalped them. Practically the entire garrison was carried across Lake Ontario and down the St. Lawrence River to Montreal."

Outside of the ruins of Fort Oswego the two men found some turnips growing in what had been the fort's vegetable garden.

"I never knew that raw turnips could taste as good as these do," said Peter. "Between these turnips and the strawberries we could keep alive in this place another week."

"Maybe that's true," said Phelps. "But I've a feeling that we had better be going and right now, too. I think we're tempting fate to stay around here any longer. We'd better wade the river, a short distance upstream, and follow along the opposite bank through the woods."

Though the water was up to their arm pits, they managed to ford the stream without having to swim. They climbed up the east bank of the river. Now they were among pine trees instead of the oak and chestnut they had found on the west side of the river. Keeping a short distance away from the bank, they followed the course of the stream until sundown. They had concluded that for the remainder of their journey they would risk travelling in the daytime and do their sleeping at night.

They had been a night and a day without sleep, and now prepared to lie down in the woods, a few feet back from the top of the river bank, but screened by the underbrush from the view of anyone passing up or down the stream. Peter Luney went over to the edge of the woods. He quickly dropped to the ground.

"What do you see?" said Phelps.

"You were right about getting away from Oswego," said Luney, "there's a dozen Indians going down the river. See if you know who they are."

Phelps joined him and cautiously peered through the brush.

"They look like some of Abbe Picquet's Iroquois to me," said Phelps, "maybe they've been on some mission to the Six Nations. They would have lifted our scalps all right had they found us down at Oswego."

"Who is Abbe Picquet?" said Peter.

"He's a French priest," said Phelps, "who has charge of a mission at La Presentation on the St. Lawrence River. It's located where the Oswegatchie River enters the St. Lawrence. De Lery left the St. Lawrence and started south from La Presentation when he and his men destroyed Fort Bull last year. It's the place from where most of the Indians come to raid the Mohawk Valley settlements."

The Indians passed quickly out of sight. Phelps now pointed to an island in the river.

"According to a Frenchman at Niagara, it was near here that Colonel Bradstreet's battoemen were ambushed," he said.

"When did that happen?" asked the Virginian.

"About two months before Montcalm captured Oswego," replied Phelps, "DeVilliers attacked the forts with only seven hundred men. Though the garrison drove off DeVilliers, he only retired to a little fort that he had built, north of the River Monsieur-le-Comte, on the eastern shore of Lake Ontario.

There Abbe Picquet's Indians left him, but they were replaced by sixty more savages, Folles Avoignes, brought to him by Marin. The third of July DeVilliers' band was again in this neighborhood. Right about where we are now they waited for Bradstreet's boatmen returning from their relief expedition to Oswego.

When the battoemen appeared there was hot fight, of which I have only heard the French account, though I know that Colonel Bradstreet, with only a handful of men, successfully fought off the French from an island in the river.

Two days later, DeVilliers was back in his fort at the east end of the lake. He carried off forty of the battoemen as prisoners.

That night, in spite of the ever-present insects, Luney and Phelps, from sheer exhaustion, slept until sunrise.

Much refreshed, they started out at once. Remembering the many bends of the river which flowed out of Oneida Lake, Phelps planned their course to the southeast, through the woods. They left the river on their right. Soon the character of the forest changed. Instead of pine, the trees were "hickory, butternut and Linwood."

At the end of the second day they reached the shore of Lake Oneida, close to where the river leaves it. During the day they had killed a porcupine with the butt end of the musket.

"This little animal," said Phelps, "is as good to eat as a little pig. He is a great find for any men without food in the woods, it's so easy to kill him with a club."

That night the travellers slept on the north shore of Oneida Lake. Early in the morning they began their journey eastward, following the shore. By nightfall, without great exertion, they were half way up the lake.

Again they had a good sleep. The next night found them at the east end of the lake, not far from the mouth of Wood Creek. Not being certain of who might come down the creek early the next morning and surprise them, they decided to spend the night in the woods away from the mouth of the stream.

The next day, which, according to their reckoning, was the second of July, the two men sat down to plan as carefully as possible the details of the remainder of their journey.

"As near as I can figure, Peter," said Phelps, "we should make Fort Herkimer or German Flats in four days of travelling. From here on we'll have to watch our steps, particularly around the Carrying Place, where they bring the battoes overland from the Mohawk River to Wood Creek.

"There were two forts there. One of them, Fort Bull, was on Wood Creek and the other, Fort Williams, near the Mohawk. Now both of them are gone. The French, led by DeLery, took Fort Bull last year late in March. After DeLery's men were inside of the fort and had killed most of the garrison, who had refused to accept quarter, the powder magazine caught fire. The French only had time to get clear of the walls when the powder exploded. We heard the three explosions way over at Oswego.

"General Webb destroyed Fort Williams last year when he heard that Montcalm had captured Oswego.

"Those Indians from the St. Lawrence River may be down in this region right now, for all we know. They frequently come by the way of the Salmon River, which the French call La Grande Famine. They enter the river from Lake Ontario, about twenty miles east of Oswego, follow it eastward for at least ten miles and then leave it for a fairly well travelled Indian trail, which leads to the Oneida village to the south of us. They leave the trail somewhere north of where we are now and head eastward for the Carrying Place.

"We certainly do not want to be surprised by any of Abbe Picquet's Indians, not when we have managed to come this far in safety. The danger will be that the clever devils will track us if they happen to cross where we've been walking. When they look at a man's track they can tell whether the man who made it is tired or not and, in fact, anything else about him which is essential for them to know. You realize that as well as I do."

"As far as I can see, we'll just have to take the chance," said the Virginian. "We certainly can't hide our tracks."

Throughout the day Luney and Phelps proceeded with considerable caution. Along their route they had to swim a deep tributary of Wood Creek. At night they hung up their clothes to dry and slept on a bed of pine needles.

About an hour before sundown on the following day they came to the ruins of Fort Bull on the bank of Wood Creek.

"Did you say that the French captured Fort Bull in March of last year?" said the Virginian to Phelps.

"Winter don't stop the French," said Phelps. "You can be sure they had no easy time getting here. They started from Montreal and came up the St. Lawrence, most of the way marching along the side of the river. The Indians from La Presentation guided them in their march south from that village. They had many streams to cross. The great river, Nigahiougoha,* which flows into the Bay of Niaoure, was too deep for them so they built rafts. They

* Black River.

waded the other streams with water often up to their hips. At night they built huts out of what material they could find in the woods.

"The garrison of seventy men in Fort Bull put up a terrific fight. The French had to hack down the gate of the fort with their hatchets and it took them an hour to do it. Even when they broke down the gate and rushed into the fort, the garrison wouldn't accept quarter. Fifty-five of them were killed in the fight, including Lieutenant Bull."

As far as Luney and Phelps could see down the creek, the trees along its banks had been felled into it, blocking the passage of battoes or any other craft.

They now followed the road towards the site of Fort Williams on the Mohawk.

"When the detachment under DeLery were on this road before their attack on Fort Bull," said Phelps as they walked along, "they had had nothing to eat for two days. About nine o'clock in the morning they captured a convoy of provisions coming from Fort Williams to Fort Bull.

"DeLery had hoped to capture the few men who were conducting the provisions without alarming the garrisons at either fort, but a negro escaped to Fort Williams, even outrunning the Indians."

When the two travellers reached the place where Fort Williams had stood, it was nearly dark and no point in going much further.

"We can take one precaution," said Phelps, "we can get into the Mohawk and walk up-stream half a mile or more until we find a good place to sleep."

This they proceeded to do. Looking down the river they saw that it, like Wood Creek, had been obstructed by trees and that the débris and drift wood brought down by high water had greatly increased the obstructions. Finding a pine thicket, they wasted no time in getting to sleep.

Next morning at sunrise they started back down the river, this time through the woods along the bank. As they were about to enter the clearing, near the ruins of Fort Williams, Phelps laid a restraining hand on Luney's arm.

Out in the clearing were no less than ten savages, who had camped there for the night.

"Those devils were following our tracks yesterday," whispered Phelps. "They must have concluded that, after we entered the river, we went down the stream."

"It's a good thing we did as we did," said Luney, "or we wouldn't be alive."

The savages soon departed, taking their route down the south side of the Mohawk.

"They are probably headed for a raid on the settlements," said Phelps.

The two fugitives were indeed in a dilemma. The savages were between them and Fort Herkimer. If they followed the Indians down the river, there was no certainty that Luney and Phelps would not meet them returning from their raid. To remain where they were was equally dangerous. They had eaten nothing for two days and there was little chance of obtaining any food unless they fired the musket and that they did not dare to do.

"The only thing that I can think of," said Phelps, "is to follow them down the river. The chances are that they will attack someone in German Flats. While they are on the north side of the river and before they recross, we can continue down the south side until we reach Fort Herkimer."

"Have you any idea where they will cross the river?" said Luney.

Phelps did not answer immediately. He was trying to visualize the course of the Mohawk between where they now were and German Flats. It was two years since he had come up the stream in a battoe. Finally he answered the Virginian.

"When we came up the river, my recollection is that they showed me a ford about ten miles this side of German Flats. That would be about twenty miles from where we are now. I would guess that the Indians would camp somewhere near the ford tonight. We can go down the river to within five miles of it and then continue on down the river in the morning."

In spite of their hunger and impatience to reach Fort Herkimer, not until nearly noon did the two men follow the route taken by the savages.

As they made their way cautiously down the river, neither one of them would have been surprised to see the Indians come pouncing out upon them. They passed every thicket, which looked like a possible cover for the savages, with the greatest relief.

When towards nightfall they estimated that they had travelled about fifteen miles, they sought the shelter of a pine thicket. The exertion of the march had greatly increased their hunger, but that was no new experience to them and unless the Indians recaptured them, they were only another day's march to safety.

In the morning they started their march an hour after sunrise. They well realized that this day's march would be the most hazardous of their entire journey. Suppose the Indians had travelled further than they had estimated, had struck a blow in German Flats and were already on their return march. Whatever had happened, they had no choice but to go forward. With the greatest caution they moved down the river.

After two hours of travelling, Phelps, who was ahead, beckoned to Luney to come forward. He pointed to the ground. There were the unmistakable footprints of the savages. They followed them to the edge of the river.

"Here is where they crossed," said Phelps.

"There's no doubt about it," said Luney.

"Now that we are satisfied as to where they are," said Phelps, "we had better get out of here and down the river as fast as we can."

With no further discussion they started off into the woods. Now they went back from the stream to the base of the hills which formed the south side of the river valley and followed along them. By the time it was nearly dark they had passed three fair-sized creeks which entered the river from the south. To obtain some idea of the progress they had made, they again approached the edge of the Mohawk.

Evidently they were not far from their destination. On the opposite side and down the stream but a short distance were some clearings. Back from them and near the base of the hills north of the river they could make out some of the buildings of the Palatines of German Flats.

"Look up the river," said Luney.

Not over half a mile away on the opposite side a cloud of thick gray smoke was visible above the trees.

"That's the work of the Indians all right," said Phelps.

They turned back from the stream and in spite of their great weakness hastened their march through the woods.

An hour after sundown they came out into a clearing and saw the fort just ahead of them. Some men about it came running out to meet them.

While they satisfied their hunger the garrison crowded around them plying them with questions as to their experiences and as to their knowledge of the plans of the French.

Upon their arrival at the fort, Luney and Phelps had informed the commandant of the fire that they had seen. A few minutes after their arrival a boy of fourteen came over the river from the German Flats side accompanied by a youth of about twenty. The boy was in a terribly excited condition. He had gone to meet his father who was working near a barn up the river. He had nearly reached it when from the edge of the clearing he had seen the Indians capture his father and fire the barn. He had run all the way back to the village and the older boy had brought him to the fort. The commandant concluded that the enemy Indians were by this time too far away to make a pursuit worthwhile.

The older Palatine youth did his best to satisfy the boy that as long as he had not seen the Indians harm his father that they would carry him off as a prisoner. Eventually he would escape or return after the war was over.

Though Phelps and Luney were well nigh exhausted from their travels with so little food, they had no desire to sleep and rather enjoyed the recital of their experiences. They could not but notice that the supply of liquor in the fort was being dispensed quite freely.

"I don't like the looks of that suttler," said Peter Luney, referring to the dealer in liquors, whom the soldiers called Tom Smith.

"Nor I, either," said Phelps.

In the fort were some Indians of the Six Nations, who were to start on a scout towards the St. Lawrence River country in the morning. Two of them had drunk more liquor than they could easily carry and were having a mild altercation with the suttler, Tom Smith, who had also imbibed too freely.

"As soon as an Indian gets one drink of liquor he immediately wants another," said Peter Luney.

About midnight a shot rang out from the room where Smith had been plying the two Indians with liquor. The soldiers, the other Indians, followed by Luney and Phelps rushed into the room. On the floor was one of the Indians with a knife in his back. The other, who had been shot, was breathing his last in a chair. Smith had run out into the night.

Fifteen minutes later the soldiers returned with the suttler. Only with the greatest difficulty were the Indians restrained from at once taking vengeance upon the now terror-stricken suttler, who was promptly placed under a strong guard.

The Indians now announced that instead of going on a scout, they would go down the river to General Johnson in the morning.

"I think we had better go along with the Indians," said Peter Luney when the two men were alone, "I don't like this place."

"Nor I," said Phelps.

In the morning they approached the Indians and found them willing to take them down the river as far as Fort Johnson.

At an hour after sunrise they began their journey. The Mohawks, who had been deeply stirred by the murder of two of their men, spoke little.

Down the beautiful valley, past the little falls where the rock cliffs were close together, the canoes sped rapidly with the powerful paddle-strokes of the Indians. Now there were occasional stone houses near the river. Farther back, on the clearings, they sighted less substantial structures of wood. They reached the Mohawk village of Canajoharie by noon. Phelps and Luney entered the village with the Indians. Here they found some troops from North Carolina, some of whom Luney had known in Virginia.

After a stop of two hours, spent by the Indians in condoling the relatives of the two murdered men, they continued their journey down the river. They had now been joined by more Indians.

By nightfall they had reached the mouth of the Schoharie Creek, where the Indian village of Fort Hunter was located on the south side of the river. Here the Indians stopped again.

It was dark when the journey was resumed. After an hour on the water the Indians beached their craft on the north bank of the river.

As they crossed a spacious lawn, extending back from the stream, they could make out the outline of a large house ahead of them.

"You are going to meet a man of great consequence in America," said Phelps to Peter Luney.

As they came nearer to the house they saw that, with some other adjoining buildings, it was surrounded by an outer wall. They were admitted at the gate and went directly to the house.

General Johnson met them at the door. Quickly the Mohawks related the affair at Fort Herkimer. It was easy to see that General Johnson was greatly disturbed at this news. Leaving the Indians for a moment, he conducted Phelps and Luney to a comfortable room, in which a fire was burning in the grate. Here he left them with his daughter, Nancy, while he went into the library with the Indians.

For the two escaped prisoners to again talk to a woman of their own people was indeed a real pleasure. Even though this daughter of General Johnson was not yet out of her teens, she had been remarkably well instructed by a private teacher.

She at once put Phelps and Luney at ease and soon had them pouring out the tales of their individual captivities, and their joint experiences since they had left Niagara.

She was horror stricken at the murder of the two Indians.

Such an affair as had occurred at Fort Herkimer, she said, would only add to the great difficulties under which, in spite of constant

English blunders and defeats, her father labored so assiduously to keep the Indians loyal to England and the Colonies.

She went on to tell them that representatives of the Six Nations were still at Fort Johnson, having just concluded a meeting with General Johnson. All the Indians would be furious at this new outrage.

For a full two hours the two men visited with Miss Nancy while General Johnson parleyed with the highly incensed Indians.

Then General Johnson took them into his library. Before he heard their stories and reports of conditions at Niagara he opened a bottle of his best wine.

General Johnson, in the first year of the war, 1755, had led the Provincial troops and his Indian allies at Lake George, where his forces had decisively beaten the French and their Indian allies under General Dieskau.

After the successful campaign of that year, General Johnson had resigned his commission. Yet he was still Colonel of the New York militia. Not only was he in charge of Indian affairs in America, but he was also the military leader of the Indians.

He raised the New York militia in any emergency, and on his expeditions was accompanied by the Indians. He kept Indian scouting parties covering the entire territory about Lake George and Lake Champlain and the country northward to the St. Lawrence River, and even westward to the region of the Ohio.

One of the Mohawks had been captured by a party of Indians from the Illinois country and taken to Fort Duquesne. Though the Indians had put him to death by a slow fire, above which they had placed the Mohawk on a hoop of green wood supported by forked sticks, this warrior had continually shouted defiance at his captors until he died.

General Johnson's home, Fort Johnson, had become the focal point of military operations on the frontier. He and his allies, the Six Nations, protected Schenectady and Albany from any attack of the French by way of the Mohawk Valley.

Right at this time the English Commander-in-Chief, Lord Loudon, had gone off to attack Louisbourg. That officer, with the many titles, had taken with him forces sorely needed on the northern frontier. General Johnson was in constant apprehension of a French attack. He was prepared to at once raise the militia to meet it.

After Phelps and Luney had related their experiences and given the General all the information that they had been able to glean from the French at Niagara, he found them suitable quarters for the night. After the two men were alone they had a chance to comment on their surroundings.

"Lord, man," said Peter Luney, "I never knew that anybody had an establishment like this way out on the frontier! Did you see the books in the library? There were histories and the lives of the great military leaders. The more one learns of General Johnson the more he grows in stature."

"That is unquestionably true," said Phelps, "and what is more, any man that can conduct himself the way he did at the Battle of Lake George must be somewhat of a military leader.

"Early in that battle while encouraging his men, General Johnson was painfully wounded in the hip. Regardless of it he took up a position on the artillery ground while his aid-de-camp, Peter Wraxall, was everywhere.

"Towards the end of the battle the enemy were pouring into a low ground from which to assault the camp. General Johnson saw the danger and, 'with all the calmness in the world,' sent the order to the officer in command of the gunners to fire some shells among them with the hoyet. It was done and the enemy was driven out of the swamp. Had the shells not been thrown the enemy would certainly have forced the camp.

"General Johnson," continued Phelps, "seems to know how to get along not only with the Indians, but with all classes of people. Most of those New Englanders at Lake George had the highest regard for the General as soon as they became personally acquainted with him.

"To be sure, some of them, principally the supporters of Governor Shirley of Massachusetts, have invented all manner of malicious stories about him. As one of our New York men has said of General Johnson's jealous detractors: 'The great celebration given by the New Yorkers in his honor "stuck in the maw of the reptiles. They couldn't digest it." ' "

After the best sleep that Phelps and Luney had enjoyed since they both had left the settlements, they ate breakfast with General Johnson and his daughter Nancy.

After providing them with funds for the remainder of their journey, that afternoon the General put them aboard a battoe that was going down the Mohawk River to Schenectady.

That night they stayed in Schenectady and had an opportunity to learn how the Dutch of that city lived.

"I had supposed," said Peter Luney next morning, "that it was only in the South that there were many negroes, but from the way these Dutchmen sit around on their porches, smoking their pipes, I'd say that the negroes do a considerable amount of the work."

As the two travellers passed through the streets they caught glimpses of the barefooted and barelegged Dutch women who occasionally left their work to appear in the doorways.

"What short dresses they do wear," said Phelps.

About noon, being by this time well accustomed to walking, they started on foot for Albany. Reaching that city about sundown, they had no trouble in finding lodgings for the night.

The activity in Albany proved to be far greater than in Schenectady. Supplies were moving up the Hudson River towards Fort Edward.

Phelps soon learned something more of the fate of Flanagan and Carter who had been captured with him at Oswego. A Lieut. Jeremiah Lincoln had made his escape from Montreal about the same time as had Luney and Phelps from Niagara. Lincoln had passed through Albany on his way to Boston from Fort Edward. At the docks were several vessels that sailed between Albany and New York.

After a wait of three days in Albany, Phelps and Luney secured passage for New York. In four days they reached the city. Phelps sought out his old employer, the ship builder, Jonas Wright. He was welcomed like one returned from the grave. The ship builder offered Phelps his former position.

Peter Luney bid Phelps farewell and started for Philadelphia.

Part 2

"Jerry Lincoln," said Captain Hodges to me on a day in mid-September, 1756, "you are to have your wish. Tomorrow about fifty of us start out on a scout down the west side of Lake George."

This was welcome news. I was heartily sick of the humdrum life at Fort William Henry. The inaction had become almost unendurable. Even mild forms of amusement such as playing cards were strictly forbidden.

Even Chaplain Graham had become tired of the daily routine. I had become quite attached to the good preacher, but there was no doubt that his services were becoming less and less popular. He seemed to take the blame for this turn of events entirely unto himself, remarking that he was of no use whatsoever about the camp.

"Why," he said to me one Sunday afternoon, "even General Lyman does not come to my services. He has told me many times how much he was opposed to the sin of profanity, yet today while I was conducting the services General Lyman was but a few feet away in another tent. With him was another officer who was cursing terribly, but General Lyman did nothing to stop him."

It was not for me to comment on Gen. Phineas Lyman. I knew that he was very devout, a strict disciplinarian and an inveterate hater of the Yorkees, as he called the New York troops. They in turn derisively referred to General Lyman as Turrenne, Louis the Fourteenth's famous General.

This was the season of the year when the shores of Lake George were most beautiful, upon this clear, cool September morning, with already some change in the color of the ripened leaves, the woods were gorgeous.

It being Sunday, we did not set out until after the morning services. By noon we were about four miles up the west shore of the lake, and had stopped to partake of the provisions that we had brought with us. It had warmed considerably during the day, so that the entire company were perspiring considerably.

Our instructions were to reconnoiter Ticonderoga and if possible to bring back two or three prisoners.

Captain Hodges had been told, before we left William Henry, that we must particularly be on our guard near Northwest Bay. Our plan was to pass around the bay, then through the mountains to the westward of Lake George.

At about one o'clock we resumed our march, two or three abreast, with Captain Hodges in the lead. We were back from the shore of the lake about a quarter of a mile, and were just passing along the base of a ledge on our left.

The forest seemed unusually quiet. I have often thought, since that time, that I had a premonition of evil and that the stillness seemed unnatural.

From somewhere up on the ledge there came the sound of a breaking twig. Captain Hodges heard it. He held up his hand to halt the men back of him. We stopped in our tracks. We had no more than done so when it seemed that all the demons and fiends that I suppose inhabit Hell were almost instantly among us.

Over the ledge they came, naked, screaming savages, painted black and red. Captain Hodges was lying dead upon the ground with his head smashed by a tomahawk in less than ten seconds. I, myself, received a glancing blow that stunned me, so that I saw nothing further of the actual combat. Only for that I would have met the same fate as most of the company.

I must have laid there, entirely bereft of my senses, for at least half an hour, and I often thank the Lord that such was the case.

When I recovered consciousness it was to see all about me the dead, naked and mutilated bodies of those who had been my companions. Their hearts and some of their other organs had been torn from their bodies. Their bleeding scalps were dangling from the waists of the fiends that now looked menacingly down upon me.

How I happened to be alive I could not understand, until I saw an immense Indian towering above me. He had evidently claimed me as his individual property. Up against the ledge were sixteen more of my companions who stood there, stark naked, with their arms tied behind their backs.

I counted the dead bodies that lay before us. With the prisoners there was a total of forty-eight. Only five of our number had managed to escape, and the savages might even have run them down in the woods.

As far as I could make out, the party that had ambushed us numbered nearly 150 Canadians and savages, over a hundred of them Iroquois of splendid physique.

I was now stripped and tied like the other prisoners. Then they led us to the shore of Lake George and put us in their canoes. Thus we started down the lake. We were undoubtedly to see Ticonderoga but certainly in a manner far different than we had intended.

We had gone but a few miles when out from the shore came many more canoes. When these came along side of us we saw that the enemy numbered in all about six hundred men.

Our scouting expedition had, unfortunately, been launched at a time when the French themselves had sent out the largest detachment that went up Lake George from Ticonderoga during that entire year.

Even though we had not been surprised at that particular time, the same fate would have undoubtedly befallen us later in the course of the day.

The savages drove their canoes down Lake George with what seemed to me incredible speed. By seven o'clock that night we were at the north end of the lake. I looked about for my companions. Half an hour later they arrived. Now instead of sixteen there were thirteen. Three of them, being already wounded, had been taken to the shore, murdered and scalped.

We had hardly arrived at the camp at the landing place when General Montcalm arrived from Ticonderoga.

To his credit, he immediately informed the savages that he would purchase us from them. That same evening we were marched to Ticonderoga. What the purchase prices for the others were, I do not know, but for me the Marquis paid my Indian captor 300 livres, the value of fifteen bushels of indian corn when food became scarce in Canada.

Now that the French had bought me from the savages, I was again properly clothed. After being provided with something to eat, I was conducted to Bougainville, Montcalm's aid-de-camp, who questioned me about the strength of our forces.

Whether he determined it from my guarded answers or those of other prisoners, I do not know. But he correctly estimated our forces at Fort William Henry at two thousand Provincials. He also knew that we had many sick.

Bougainville informed me that the next day I would be sent down Lake Champlain to Montreal, also that Montcalm had succeeded in purchasing most of our men from the savages, so that they were now safe and would follow me to Montreal. I was confined alone that night.

Next morning at daybreak I was put in custody of three Canadians whom I was to accompany on my journey down the lake. To my surprise the savages were already leaving for the north. The Ottawas went off with four of my

companions.   A little later nearly 400 more
savages launched their canoes on Lake Champlain and headed north.   There were now but
a few Indians left at Ticonderoga.

A little before noon I boarded a bark boat
with the three Canadians.   They were not at all
unfriendly and fortunately I knew a little
French.

As we approached Crown Point late in the
afternoon I was much surprised at the appearance of the surrounding country.   I had expected to see a fort, entirely enclosed by the
forest.   Instead for a short distance back from
the shore, and on both sides of the lake, were
farm lands.

Crown Point had been settled for some time.
Some of the French settlers, mostly old soldiers,
still cultivated the fields and before the war had
raised unusually good crops.

The Canadians beached their craft and we
went on shore.   As soon as we had eaten we
again started down the lake.   I took a hand at
the oars and was surprised at the speed that we
were able to make in the bark boat.

Not far north of Crown Point we passed a
convoy of about thirty large boats coming up

the lake loaded with provisions and supplies for Ticonderoga.

It was evidently the intention of my escort to take advantage of the brisk south wind and go just as far down the lake that night as possible; we continued our journey for three or four hours after it was dark. Around midnight we reached the outlet of Otter Creek, on the east side of the lake. This stream the French call La Loutre.

My hands had not been tied, and I was given to understand that they would not be if I would agree not to attempt to escape. Such an attempt seemed futile, at least at this time. So I was entirely agreeable to the arrangement.

Again we were away at daylight. Now a head wind had sprung up, and our progress was not so rapid as on the previous night. About two hours after we were under way we passed a huge rock on the west shore of the lake which seemed to be split asunder from the northern tip of the mountain spur on that side of the lake.

Noticing that I was intently observing this formation, the Canadians volunteered the information that it was the Rocher-Fendu, and formerly the northern limit of the lands of the Six Nations.

Beyond this split rock the lake immediately widened. Here the water was much rougher and I had some misgivings as to the safety of the boat. All four of us were now at the oars and it required all our strength and skill to keep the craft from capsizing. Six or seven miles north of split rock the Canadians pointed out the mouth of the Bouquet River, a stream entering the lake from the west.

We stopped not at all at noon. For safety's sake we remained as close as possible to the west shore of the lake. At what I estimated at two hours past mid day we passed four little islands on our right, known to the French as the Iles of the Four Winds. About two hours before sundown we beached the craft on Schuyler Island.

By this time the wind had gone down and the weather had turned unusually warm. So we slept in the open in the woods.

Next morning we again started out at daybreak. I had learned by this time that nearly all Canadian and French expeditions started at dawn or earlier, a custom which I could not but observe would not be a bad one to adopt universally among the English and Colonial troops.

Now the lake had widened greatly and it seemed to extend more than ten miles from shore to shore.   There was no heavy wind or we could not have continued without considerable danger of capsizing.   We passed another river on our left, called by the Canadians, the Ausable.   That night we slept on a sandy beach along the south side of a point which projected out into the lake from the western shore.

The lake had greatly narrowed again, or I should properly say had been split in twain, so to speak, by several large islands which were apparently not far apart.   We were in the western portion of the lake.

Hardly were we under way next morning when we saw some canoes approaching from the north, in which I counted eighteen savages. They brought their craft along side of us.   The Indians were certainly of a tribe that I had never seen.   Only one of the Canadians could talk their language.   After they had passed he informed us that the Indians were Pouteotamis from the neighborhood of far-off Detroit.

That day we made more rapid progress than on any preceding one.   By four o'clock St. Johns was in sight to the northward.

At night I slept in a bed.   Though I was a prisoner, I was not being ill treated, and in fact, enjoyed the same habitation and the same food as these Canadians. I shuddered to think of how I might have been faring had not the Marquis de Montcalm purchased me from the savages.

Again at dawn next morning we started for Montreal and on foot. When I saw the road that we had to traverse I was just as well satisfied that we were walking. I had seen many wet and rutted roads but never one like this one. It was nothing but a succession of deep ruts and puddles of water. It would have in places been almost impassable were it not for logs and branches that had been laid crosswise to the line of travel.

By the middle of the afternoon we had left the woods and swamps behind us and were among cultivated farm lands. Here were good growing crops, everything that I had ever seen in New York and New England.

By two hours before sundown we were in the village of La Prairie and a few minutes later on the bank of the St. Lawrence River. On the other side of the river was the city of Montreal, its buildings visible above the low wall that surrounded it.

As we crossed the river in a battoe, I began to wonder what the jails in that city were like and how long I would have to remain in one of them.

Even though I was a prisoner, I was very curious to see the city of Montreal, whose buildings I could now make out in the distance. From all accounts they were a brave people who dwelt within its walls. They loved to hunt and would go on long voyages with the savages, constantly singing as they plied their fragile craft through dangerous waters. While they might make plenty of money from a successful voyage they would be very quick to spend it. On the other hand, the people of Quebec were supposed to be more interested in trading. The inhabitants of Montreal referred to the citizens of Quebec as sheep and the people of Quebec retaliated by calling the people of Montreal wolves.

Our entrance into the city caused almost no attention. It was obvious to the people on the streets that I was not French and must therefore be a prisoner. Evidently the inhabitants had seen so many English prisoners that one more was no curiosity. I was impressed by the attractive appearance of the women in their high-heeled shoes, short skirts and gay little jackets. Their animated faces showed their abundant vitality.

When we reached the jail I was taken to a solitary room. To my great surprise the Canadian said to me:

"I'll be back in the morning. You can then go and find some other English prisoners. They will probably help you find work. We can't afford to keep you in the jail because we haven't the food to give you." This was news indeed. My lot in Montreal was to be far different than I had contemplated. I was to work and support myself.

True to his promise, the Canadian came next morning to the jail and released me.

"I will take you to Colonel Schuyler," he said. "The Colonel has made it his particular business to look after all the English prisoners in Montreal."

I had heard of Col. Peter Schuyler and I knew that his regiment of Jersey Blues had, for the most part, been captured with him at Oswego on the 14th of August.

The Canadian conducted me to Colonel Schuyler's residence and left me with the Colonel. I knew at once that I had found a friend. Most naturally he wanted to know the latest news of affairs to the southward. To say that it grieved him to hear of the fate of our scouting party on Lake George would be to put it mildly.

After he had told me something of the life and possible occupations of English prisoners in Montreal he said to me:

"It is not impossible that I can get something for you to do with a boat builder down on the river. We might as well go down there now."

When we reached the river we found several prisoners already employed at the building of battoes. Their French overseer in common with most of the inhabitants of Montreal seemed to have a very friendly attitude towards Colonel Schuyler. The overseer immediately put me to work with two men who had lately arrived from Niagara.

They were James Flanagan of New Jersey and Charles Carter of Philadelphia. That night they took me to their abiding place where I found it possible to make arrangements to stay myself.

That evening they related to me their own experiences.

"With two other men, William Phelps and Lewis Dunning, we were cutting ship timber outside of the forts of Oswego," said Flanagan.

"About the middle of last June we, like many before us, were captured by the savages that were constantly lurking about the forts. They started us off for Niagara with them.

"Poor Dunning," continued Flanagan, "he was wounded and did not travel fast enough to suit the Indians, so one of them hit him on the head with a tomahawk.

"I'll never forget the way the savage took Dunning's scalp. He turned him over on his face, cut his scalp with his knife, then with one foot planted between Dunning's shoulders and with that bloody knife between his teeth, with both hands he ripped off the scalp.

"When we reached Niagara the Indians carried off Phelps to their country and we were sent across Lake Ontario and down the St. Lawrence to Montreal."

Carter and Flanagan were most congenial company. A few days after my arrival the rest of my companions in our ill fated expedition reached Montreal and also found employment.

My stay in Montreal was marked by no unusual occurrences. The chief topic of our conversation was the probable future course of the war. We learned considerable from the French soldiers and also from the English prisoners who were being constantly brought to Montreal.

It was a matter of common knowledge in this French city that there was little harmony between the French governor and the Marquis de Montcalm. The Governor General was evidently extremely jealous of the success of Montcalm at Oswego. However, there was no antagonism on the part of the Governor General to General Levis, second in command to Montcalm.

Early in '57 we began to hear rumors of a winter expedition against Fort William Henry. This was to be under the command of Rigaud de Vaudreuil, brother of the Governor General. Montcalm was not even to be consulted about the proposed undertaking. General Levis had strongly advised the Governor General against making the expedition, telling him that it would not be successful.

Shortly after the middle of February, Rigaud and sixteen hundred men departed for the South. They were most thoroughly equipped for such an expedition. I was more than apprehensive that the garrison of Fort William Henry would be surprised and that the fort would be taken.

In January seventy-seven Rangers under Capt. Robert Rogers had captured some men conducting sleds between Ticonderoga and Crown Point. Those of the French who had escaped hot-footed it for Ticonderoga. Captain Rogers led the return march of the Rangers by the same route that they had taken in reaching Lake Champlain. A party of the garrison at Ticonderoga surprised the Rangers, killed forty-two of them and took eight prisoners.

The New Hampshire man, John Stark, had distinguished himself in this affair.

I feared a fate similar to Rogers' men for the garrison at Fort William Henry. I was prepared to see the savages that accompanied Rigaud return with the scalps of my friends.

Not until April did the news of this expedition reach Montreal. Then I heard the story from a French regular who had no love for Rigaud.

"Ten days it took them," the soldier said, "to go over the ice from St. Johns to Crown Point. The dogs drew their supplies. The soldiers slept on bear skins in their tents. They tried to surprise the garrison of Fort William Henry in the middle of the night, but a sentry heard them out on the ice. After they had succeeded in burning some buildings and boats around the fort, Rigaud's men retired to their camp a short distance down Lake George.

"After a wait of a day or two they marched up the lake again towards the fort. To intimidate the garrison, Rigaud had his men spread way out across the lake. They held up their scaling ladders, hoping to scare the garrison. Rigaud now sent a summons to the fort, demanding a surrender. It met with no success.

"M. Wolf distinguished himself two days later by burning the last remaining vessel. With twenty volunteers he went right up close to the fort. In spite of the hot fire from the fort, which killed two of our men and wounded another, M. Wolf piled wood up against the vessel. When he tried to fire the wood it was too big, so he split it with his hatchet and ignited it. The fire completely destroyed the barge.

"By this time Rigaud had come to the conclusion that the fort could not be captured by assault. He therefore ordered his soldiers to march back down the lake. They made their way to Ticonderoga and back down Lake Champlain. At the north end of the lake it had become so warm that they had to use battoes to reach St. Johns.

"To be sure," continued the soldier, "Rigaud's men destroyed 300 battoes and four barges at Fort William Henry, but he didn't take the fort. The cost of the expedition was too great. The ill success of it should teach the Governor General in the future to leave the conduct of military affairs to his generals." This good news of the failure of the attack on Fort William Henry was followed by reports of a proposed attack on that fort with practically all the French military resources in Canada and under the leadership of the Marquis de Montcalm and General Levis. If this happened, I had no doubt that William Henry would fall and possibly Fort Edward.

Not only were the so-called domesticated savages allied with the French to go on this expedition, but the savage tribes from the far west about the Great Lakes. On the 13th of June several hundred of these savages came into Montreal from far-off Michillimakinac.

During the long Canadian winter I had become acquainted with most of the prisoners in the city. One of them, a British regular who had been captured at Oswego, and my two friends, Carter and Flanagan, had suggested to me several times that we try to escape. They had advanced the idea to me because I had obtained some knowledge of the country when I was brought down Lake Champlain as a prisoner.

When I saw those savages coming in from the West I made up my mind that if we were to escape at all, that we had better make the attempt before any more French and Indians occupied the region about Ticonderoga and Crown Point.

The four of us immediately made our plans. We would cross the St. Lawrence River and then strike south through the woods. When we were well past the low swampy country in the vicinity of the Isle au Noix, we would return as near as we dared to the west shore of Lake Champlain and continue our course southward along it.

On the night of June 14th we took a boat at the edge of the St. Lawrence River in front of the city and set out for the south shore. We had one gun and about twenty rounds of powder and ball. Our provisions consisted of fifteen pounds of pork. No one was astir in La Prairie as it was at least two hours after midnight. We followed the road to St. Johns for about a mile, then struck south through the fields for a short distance and then into the woods. Fortunately it was not too dark a night. We wanted to go as far as possible before daylight and I estimated that we had covered six miles before the first trace of light appeared in the east.

It would have been the height of folly for us to rest even though we had had no sleep. We kept on until finally late in the afternoon we were forced to sleep from sheer exhaustion.

For six days with the sun as our guide we travelled southward through the woods and without attempting to approach Lake Champlain. We were not sure how far west we were from it.

When I had come down the lake as a prisoner in the previous year I had noted the mountains which were along the western shore as far as the Ausable River. We had not yet reached them.

We had crossed several streams and though it had been hazardous in many places we had not yet been forced to swim. Our pork was gone but we had had the good luck to kill two porcupines and had not suffered from hunger. We had seen considerable game, including a moose. However, we did not think it wise to shoot the musket in this region at least until we knew that we were a safe distance from Lake Champlain.

At the end of the sixth day we came to a river which I concluded must be the Ausable. We had seen mountains not far to the southward of it.

At the point where we had reached this stream it flowed through a most beautiful and unusual gorge, or chasm, with vertical sides. To cross here was out of the question. We went about two miles up stream along the bank of this beautiful river and then had to swim to cross it.

As it was nearly dark after we had crossed, we took off our clothes and went to sleep in the pines at the top of the bank. In spite of the insects, which did their best to keep us from it, we slept soundly until dawn.

Before we had crossed this river we had caught sight of a hill to the southeast which seemed to rise four or five hundred feet above the plain that was immediately south of the river. We now determined to climb this hill and from its top see if we could determine our location.

In less than an hour we were upon a bare rock at the top of it. What a sight met our eyes. To the west and south were mountains. To the north was the forested low country which stretched off towards Montreal, whence we had come. To the northeast was Lake Champlain, miles and miles of it. A portion of it was hidden from view by a mountain mass between us and the lake, but to the right of this towards the southeast more of the lake was visible. We were evidently at about the widest part of the lake and I estimated that it was ten miles or more across it. I could make out the four little islands that I had passed with the three Canadians. We did not dare stay where we were any longer, for out upon the lake we thought we could make out the boats of the French or the savages.

Our climb had well repaid us, for now we knew where we were. The remainder of the journey would have to be planned with considerable care. The closer we approached to Crown Point and Ticonderoga the greater would be the chance of our being discovered.

From our present location it was not over three miles to the edge of Lake Champlain, yet for the present it seemed wise to keep away from it.

To the southward were the mountains. A little to the westward of what we estimated to be directly south, there was apparently a pass through them, flanked on the west side by a nearly vertical cliff several hundred feet in height. We decided to make for it. On the other side of the notch it was more than likely that by following a stream we could again approach Lake Champlain.

Keeping to the left of the two little lakes that were between us and the notch, we were able to reach the base of the cliff. Shortly after noon here we ate the last of the two porcupines and were now entirely out of provisions.

As I had expected, after we had gone southward about a mile further we found a brook. This we decided to follow until we were again near Lake Champlain.

Following this stream was not easy as there was considerable underbrush along its course. After we had travelled what seemed to be six or seven hours we stopped for the night. We had seen nothing to shoot so we went to sleep hungry.   We would soon be in a neighborhood in which it would not be safe to risk the sound of the gun.   If we were to shoot anything it was best to do it before we were again close to Lake Champlain.

Of my three companions the British regular from Oswego was the youngest.   Both Flanagan and Carter had no surplus flesh to draw from. The tall, red-headed Flanagan was now mostly skin and bones.   Carter was small and wiry. Flanagan, I could see, had a great affection for him.   The three of them were excellent companions, yet how long we could go without food was a problem.

I was awakened next morning by the noise of some animal crashing through the brush. Cautiously I reached for the musket and waited. In another minute a fair-sized deer appeared about a hundred and fifty feet away.   I put the musket to my shoulder and fired.

The animal gave one great leap and lay still. My companions, who had been sound asleep, jumped to their feet with startled exclamations. When I told them what I had shot they did not resent the rude awakening.   It did not take us long to dress the animal.   We decided to cook its four quarters before we went any further.

In the best of spirits, shortly before noon we resumed our journey. We now had enough food for several days.

After we had followed the brook for three or four miles it entered a much larger stream, in fact a small river, which apparently flowed east. We entered the bed of it and for three or four miles walked in the water.

Directly ahead of us was an open space and to our surprise our stream joined a river flowing north. This I could not quite understand, for surely we must be near Lake Champlain. I concluded that it must be the Bouquet and that it soon turned in its course towards the lake.

We decided to leave the river and strike eastward for the lake. About sundown we could see its shining surface through the trees ahead of us. Not daring to approach closer we slept that night in the woods back about a quarter of a mile from the lake.

Next morning I decided to risk a visit near to the shore. To my relief no craft of any sort was in sight.   Down the lake, seven or eight miles to the northward, were the four little islands.   In the opposite direction to the south was the mountain spur that terminated in the split rock.   We were now four or five miles to the northward of it.   As far as I could remember the distance from the split rock to Crown Point would be nearly twenty miles by water.

I went back to my three companions, told them where we were and what I had remembered of the country on the west side of the lake between where we now were and Crown Point.

We decided to follow along the shore, staying back about a quarter of a mile, until we reached the mountain spur that terminated in split rock. We began our march.   After we had ascended the ridge we followed along its top parallel to the lake.

About the middle of the afternoon we came to an open place where there were nothing but bare rocks.   It was a remarkably clear day and though it was apparently about fifteen miles away we could make out the outlines of what unquestionably was the fort at Crown Point. We continued three or four miles further, and coming to the end of the ridge, slept that night about half a mile back from the edge of a large bay of the lake.

The next day we travelled about eight miles. We were in a rough, rocky country that evidently was of that same nature for several miles ahead of us.

Next day we made only five miles and spent the night on the slope directly opposite Crown Point. Now we were proceeding with the utmost caution.

We started next morning at daybreak. As we dared not go closer to the water, we were obliged to work our way along the steep slope. When about noon we were at the end of the bay, Carter suddenly uttered a sharp cry of pain. There he was with one leg jammed in a crevice in the rocks that had been concealed by some low leafy bushes.

With some difficulty we extricated his leg. Carter's face was contorted in agony. There could be no doubt about what had happened. When his leg went down, the forward motion of the upper part of his body had snapped the bone just below the knee. This was indeed a tragedy.

With splinters of wood and strips of cloth torn from our shirts, we did the best we could by him. Then his boon companion, the tall, red-headed Flanagan, hoisted him upon his back as on we went.

I was surprised at the reserve of strength in that gaunt and lean body of Flanagan. Against Flanagan's protest the Britisher and myself took our turns at carrying Carter. It was no easy matter either for the injured man or for us.

Progressing with the greatest difficulty along the steep slope, we at last arrived at a point just west of the southern end of the bay that, for two miles, flanks the western side of the Crown Point peninsula. Here we descended to the base of the slope and stopped to rest. We laid Carter on some pine needles.

Flanagan sat for some time in silence with his head in his hands. He was evidently debating something within himself. Finally he spoke: "With good luck we'll be in Fort Edward in a week or ten days. With bad luck we may not reach there at all. To travel fast is out of the question.

"If the Indians discover us they may kill us then and there, or if they decide to make us prisoners they never will bother with Carter. As soon as they see that broken leg they'll hit him on the head just as they did with poor Dunning last year when they captured us at

Oswego.   Dunning could still travel but not fast enough to suit the savages.   Carter can't travel at all.

"There is only one thing to do and that is for me to take Carter into Crown Point.   The two of us will give ourselves up to the French.   Then one of their surgeons can properly set Carter's leg.   When he is well enough to be moved the French will send us both back to Montreal. Sometime there'll be an exchange of prisoners."

We had listened in silence to what Flanagan had said.   After all, he was right.   Any other course seemed suicidal.

The Britisher and I accompanied Flanagan and Carter as far as the edge of the clearing about the fort at Crown Point.   After we had seen some French soldiers come out to meet them we hastily made our way to the southward, hoping that no savage would accidentally come across our tracks.

That night we slept by a swift stream that came down out of the mountains, where we estimated that we were at least two miles west of Lake Champlain.

It was probable that we were now about ten miles north of Ticonderoga. I had thought considerably of how we could pass through that region without being discovered, and I had not yet determined how we could do so in safety.

I knew the French and their savages were camped along the outlet of Lake George. They were quite apt to have scouting parties out in many directions. I would never forget what had happened when we had run afoul of one of them last September.

Whether by reason of what had happened to us on the west side of Lake George or not, I do not know, but I had a strong feeling that we should attempt to reach Fort Edward by passing through the mountains that separated Lake George from Lake Champlain. Yet to do this we would have to first cross the outlet of Lake George. A man might as well expect to step on a nest of hornets without being stung as to try to cross that stream without being discovered.

Very cautiously we proceeded that day. Towards night we had to admit that we did not know just where we were or how close we were to the Lake George outlet.

We had just come out of a pine thicket when out from behind a tree stepped an Indian directly in our path. He held up his hand. Never, unless you have had such an experience, can you imagine the feeling of relief that came over me. This savage was none other than the famous Mohawk chief, Little Cornelius, whom I had known at Fort William Henry. He had not recognized me because of my beard, but from our appearance and the manner in which we were travelling he had known at once that we were escaped prisoners. When I had told the Britisher the identity of the Indian he was as jubilant as I had been.

It was Cornelius who, in the battle of Lake George, had fought beside a Provincial whose gun had been put out of commission by a French bullet. The Mohawk had given the man his own gun, jumped the breastwork, wrested a gun from one of the enemy, killed him and returned to fight beside the astonished Provincial.

With the Mohawk chief as a guide we continued our journey. How he accomplished it,

I don't know, but while it was still light we forded the outlet and crossed the path that led from the sawmill to the portage. We had gone but a hundred yards into the woods when, there ahead of us, waiting for Cornelius were nine more Mohawks.

There we were, just off the path travelled constantly by the enemy, and only four or five hundred feet from their tents. We supposed, of course, that the Indians would move further south for the night, for surely they were in a dangerous position.

No movement was made in this direction, and we finally realized that these Mohawk warriors intended to remain all night right under the noses of the French.

I had heard in Montreal that the Iroquois were the bravest of all the Indian nations. Now I could not but think that the Mohawks were the bravest of the brave. Certainly all that I had heard of their conduct at the battle of Lake George and their continual scouting expeditions bore out that opinion.

At daybreak next morning the five Indians stealthily took a position in a thicket close to the path frequented by the enemy.

As neither I nor my companion had a gun, we were obliged to watch what was to take place. We did not have long to wait.

A detachment of French Grenadiers came along the path. The Indians fired one volley and sprang forward. Before the French had time to sense what had happened, the Mohawks had lifted the scalps of two dead Grenadiers.

Now all of us were off to the southward at top speed. The firing of the Indians' muskets would, of course, arouse the entire camp. The enemy savages would soon be in pursuit.

The Mohawks had already carefully planned their escape from that dangerous neighborhood. With seemingly incredible speed we moved into the mountains between the north end of Lake George and that narrow portion of Lake Champlain, south of Ticonderoga.

After we had passed two mountains the Indians slowed in their pace. At what I estimated to be about ten miles south of Ticonderoga we camped for the night.

Next day we were off an hour before day-break. Though the Indians knew every foot of the way, they were extremely cautious and appeared to be in no great haste.

We had been travelling for some time not over a half mile to the westward of Lake Champlain. Toward the middle of the afternoon we began to climb along the course of a brook that came down off the mountains.

After we had made our way over numerous rock ledges to a height of nearly a thousand feet above Lake Champlain, we camped on the west shore of a small lake which was apparently about a mile in length and a quarter of a mile in width.

The Indians picked a location for our camp, such that if by any chance we were followed by a party of the enemy it was evident that some of them would die at our first fire, for we were perfectly ambushed.

Next morning we left the little lake behind us. About two miles beyond it we crossed another mountain brook and took a course to the southwest. On our left in the distance was a deep valley, we could see the mountains beyond it. Little Cornelius informed me that we had veered westward in our course in order to round the bay which extends for four or five miles to the southwest.

The Mohawks proceeded slowly enough and even more cautiously than before. They seemed to feel that some large party of the enemy was in the neighborhood.

At night we camped along another brook and about half a mile from the extreme southern end of South Bay, where General Dieskau had landed in September '55, preceding his attack on our army at the south end of Lake George.

That night it was bright moonlight. We laid out on the ground as before; for some reason I could not sleep.

As I lay there looking up at the stars the sound of distant musket shots suddenly came echoing and re-echoing from the mountain sides of the bay. Instantly the Indians were awake and on their feet.

Something was happening down the bay. From the continual firing it was unquestionably an engagement of some consequence.

There was no longer any sleep among us. For a few minutes we listened to the fusilade, and then the Indians decided that it would be better that we push on immediately towards Fort Edward. It soon would be dawn. We continued our journey southward through the mountains, following the route that Dieskau had taken two years before. As we marched continuously all that day, before dark we arrived at Fort Edward.

When we reached the fort we found the garrison in a considerable state of excitement. I was at once warmly greeted by some of the Boston men. The Britisher was immediately seized upon by some of his old companions. They soon made the both of us comfortable.

The excitement in the camp was because of the news brought in by a messenger who had come from Capt. Israel Putnam. The Captain, with less than seventy men, had ambushed two hundred and twenty-five Indians and ten Frenchmen, officers and cadets on east bay of Lake Champlain and about a mile from the lake and four or five miles from where we had spent the previous night. That was the firing we had heard. General Lyman with a relief force had already marched off towards Fort Ann.

About two hours after our arrival, Captain Putnam and his men came marching into camp.

At a point where the sides of east bay were steep rocks and only a few rods apart, Captain Putnam and his little band had laid in wait for the savages for four or five days.

At last, about three o'clock in the morning, in the bright moonlight, the enemy had appeared. Captain Putnam's men held their fire until the enemy's boats were opposite their place of concealment. Then they had poured buckshot into them and their battoes. The fight had continued until near daylight without the enemy being able to land. Then, having exhausted their ammunition, Captain Putnam and his men stole away and marched to Fort Edward. They had killed or wounded a great many of the enemy and successfully ambushed a force over three times their own strength. A great fighter was this Connecticut man, Israel Putnam.

The commanding officer at Fort Edward was the English General Webb. That I would see any fighting was most improbable. If Montcalm appeared before Fort William Henry, it was probable that Webb would retreat down the Hudson. I was under no obligation to serve, for in the previous year I had only enlisted for that year.

As for my companion, the British regular, he had already been informed that he must remain at Fort Edward.

After I had removed my considerable beard and slept one night in comfort, I was ready to depart down the Hudson to Albany and thence overland to Boston, to remain there for a little time before I again joined the Provincial army.

In the middle of the next morning I boarded a battoe for Albany. I reached there the next day. Then I started out on horseback. The second day thereafter I was in the green woods and well on my way towards Boston.